F

FROM A G.E.D. TO A C.E.O.

Carolyn Milton

or email Author at: carolynmilton14@gmail.com

ISBN-: 9781095654538

Book Cover design by Crystal Pitts/Crystal Clear Creations
Book Cover back by Kindle Publishing

Printed by Kindle Publishing., in the United States of America.

First printing edition 2019.

From a G.E.D. to a C.E.O

CONTENTS

From a G.E.D. to a C.E.O

WORDS OF ENCOURAGEMENT TO THE AUTHOR

Passion is what you will experience as you read Carolyn's journey in this book "From GED to CEO". Carolyn's passionate smile and personality is created from what resides in her soul. Her passion for serving, passion for life, and for people is contagious. You will experience her ability to win despite insurmountable odds. It is passion that ignites her possibilities into realities. Thank you Carolyn.
-Gena P. Taylor

I believe in the sun even if it isn't shining. I believe in love even when I'm alone. I believe in God even when He is silent". Carolyn this is just the beginning for the greatness God has for you, serving is your passion and your smile is needed in this world.

Love you dearly, Thea.

It's all because of God!

-Renee Reynolds

SPECIAL THANKS TO
MY LOVING MOTHER, MS. C. REYNOLDS, MY SISTER DORA SHEPPARD, MRS. CANDACY KING, MRS. CRYSTAL PITTS, AND HWLC EMPIRE

STAGE ONE

BOSS UP! & BOSSED UP!

The words that we remember the most seem to be the ones that always guide our thinking. Words of encouragement, shifts us to higher thinking. Words full of discouragement tear us down. I can remember the words I heard a man of God speak during a time when I needed a word of encouragement. He said, "Use what God has placed in your hands and open your business". I sat there listening to his words and as he spoke I looked at my hands, and realized they were created to help. I love to assist and help others in ways that bring joy and love into their lives. I knew for a long time that I was a caregiver. A caregiver is someone who gives care to others. It brings a sense of accomplishment that I can make a difference in the lives of others through doing what I love the most.

What we enjoy doing the most should be the territory we dominate with purpose and passion. I remember when I once worked for a company called Griswold's. I would give my best effort to this company because I enjoyed what I was doing. I gave all of what I knew Carolyn could give and provided my assistance for this company. Never did I slack on the job. I learned the power of reaping through serving others. I would work for others like I would want others to work if it was my company. When we intentionally give our best while working under others, we should do what we love as if we are doing it for God. It helps to remember that what we do, God has given us the ability to do it.

In the years ahead as I was growing and enjoying my passion of helping others I learned a few things from my sister Renee. She once ran a Homecare Agency in Charleston, South Carolina. I would help her out on the weekends when my workload was low in Savannah, so I was happy to assist her. I learned through this process that at times you have to go out of your region or to do what you need to do to provide for your family. I was married at that time and had provisions being made, but I never sat and waited for others to provide for me. I wanted God to continue to make a way so that I can provide for my household as well. I learned I was built to lead. I never just sat back and said I don't make a difference or that I don't matter. Always remember that God can take your little gift and turn it around for his glory for the world to see. God called me for greatness just as he is calling you. I had to realize that it was time for me to "Boss Up".

I remember working in Hilton Head, South Carolina in Sea Pines for a minimum of $54 a day. I never complained or grumbled. I did what I could do with a grateful heart. It was a rewarding experience to me. I knew someone was being blessed because of the gift of God in me. I remembered getting on the floor and rubbing one of my client's feet. While I tended to his feet, He told me that I was a very special and good person. He thanked me for helping him. I thank God he placed inside of me the ability to be humble and help others in this manner. I also worked for a company called Care South. This company served clients that other caregivers would not go to and this didn't bother me because it was something in me that loved it. I wanted to be the solution to the problem where others would not serve.

One of my coworkers would pick me up on Saturday's to assist her with one of her clients from this establishment. She was afraid of going in the home of this particular client. I was not afraid. I have always been a dare devil, as nothing seemed to give me fear, especially if my heart was in it to help others.

There are times where others would see your gift before you see the gift inside of you. I didn't understand this but God would always send someone along to confirm what was in me. I recalled this young lady by the name of Sarah. She would tell me, "Carolyn please help me get a job". I would say to myself why does this child keep asking me about a job that I didn't have for anyone at that time. I didn't know this then, but Sarah was speaking life into me as a business owner. Later in life I believed what Sarah was saying to me and she became one of my employees. God will always confirm His word and allow His word to manifest in our lives.

I remember another co-worker who worked at Grisworld, who would tell me, "Carolyn I see you owning your company one day". I could not see me owning a company back then. I didn't believe in myself and didn't think I could establish or own a company at that time. Once I began to think and believe in myself I started speaking in my own life. The more I would stand on God's word everything began to unfold before my eyes. I would tell myself, "You got this".

The first thing any of us could do to accomplish something is to first believe in ourselves and put God first in our lives. God will always will make a liar out of those who didn't believe in you and have spoken the opposite of who you are. This also applies to the inner self that could be full of doubt that causes us to not believe in ourselves. You have to "trust the process" and let God make, mold and form you into who he has called you to be. God has a way of making you great before your own eyes and any naysayers that have spoken against you.

Let the call of God on your life be great. Use the gift you have obtained from him for his Kingdom. It is now time to "Boss Up" to what God called you for in this season. I recently wrote my first book. I don't take it for granted even until this day how I marketed my books and was selling my books out of my car. I had to believe in myself and have faith in God. Faith is the substance of all miracles. Faith is the element that fuels prayer. You have to practice what you believe. I have learn to believe in myself and I ignore negative mindsets and comments. Faith is a state of mind that I chose to be a part of . Always have faith in yourself.

I put my faith in action by visiting a store with a hand full of my books. I believed that God was going to give me favor with the owner of this store to help me sell my book in his store. I asked the owner and he said just give me the books and you can place them in my store. It was my belief system that opened the door and the kind gentleman who showed me favor. So don't just think it, you have to speak it, act upon it and it will manifest so you can Boss Up!

STAGE ONE (LEVEL UP) BECOMING A "BOSS"

The definition of a "Boss" is someone who is self-made and ambitious enough, to lead and own their work.

Do you desire to be a Boss? If so, what is your work, your desires and do you have an entrepreneur mindset? List your desires and how you will succeed in becoming the Boss you have always wanted to be?

1. My Passions that I love and enjoy doing.

   a.____________________________________

   b.____________________________________

   c.____________________________________

   d.____________________________________

   e.____________________________________

2. What is it that you see yourself doing the most as it relates to serving others?

a.____

b.____

c.____

d.____

e.____

3. Who inspires you?

a.____

b.____

c.____

d.____

e.____

4. How much money do you believe it will take to fund your business?

a.____

b.____

c.____

d.____

e.____

5. What are the dreams and aspirations that you desire to accomplish?
   a.____

   b.____

   c.____

   d.____

   e.____

6. Do you have a team of Boss men/women that support and undergird you? If so who are they? Name them below.

   a.____

   b.____

   c.____

   d.____

   e.____

7. How many streams of income will your dreams produce for you? Name them and believe.

   a.____

   b.____

   c.____

   d.____

   e.____

Let's make the "crabs in a bucket" mentality a myth. Let's be together, reason together, support each other and find ways to work together. There is enough success out there for everyone. Together everyone achieves more.

-Van Johnson

STAGE TWO

SELF-CONFIDENCE

You gain strength, courage, and confidence by every experience in which you really stop to look fear in the face. You are able to say to yourself, 'I lived through this horror. I can take the next thing that comes along."

- Eleanor Roosevelt

Confidence is so very important in order to achieve success. Confidence is like knowing the moment you pull a sturdy chair out to take a seat. The chair is made to hold you. You are confident that you won't fall to the floor. Having self-confidence means believing in yourself just as much as you believe in the craftsmanship of the creator of the chair. God created us and he has given us the spirit of confidence to believe in ourselves as His Spirit lives within us.

I suffered many years from low self-esteem. I graduated with a G.E.D. and was told that I wasn't pretty enough or smart enough. The abusive relationship that I was involved in lowered my self-esteem and I thought that was love. Sometimes, I would listen to the voices in my head telling me these same negative thoughts. There were years that I would walk in a room with my head down, lacking self-confidence and low self-esteem. I remembered what a woman of God said to me about holding my head down. She said for me to hold my head up and remember that I was a child of God. She said I was to never hold my head down in front of people. When she spoke these words over my life, I felt like a million dollars. I also made a connection with a sister in Christ who told me to walk with my shoulders back. She said to me that I had to learn to practice good posture. I learned through these ladies the way I should carry myself in confidence. We have to be thankful that God will place the right people around us in our time of need. God will place the right people in our lives to help make and develop us into who He has called us to be. Some people are sent into our lives to teach us things that we need to learn about ourselves. This maybe their purpose for connecting with us. From then until now, I love to walk with my head up and my shoulders back. It's a sign of self-confidence. I learned there is a difference from being arrogant and having self-confidence. I learned that it's not arrogance when we come to know who we are in Christ. Once the revelation of who we are in Christ is revealed, it's a beautiful feeling on the inside.

I meditate thirty minutes a day and think on positive thoughts daily. I intentionally say that I will not be jealous or envious of someone else's success. I have made a self-decision that I will encourage, uplift and help others walk in their calling. I believe when we do this it will cause you to walk in self- confidence within your own life. Uplifting others will keep jealousy from arising within yourself and it builds joy and celebration within your own heart. I had to believe in myself just as much as I believed and pushed others. This is how I learned to become a business owner. Success for me as it relates to business ownership did not happen overnight. I had to learn over the years to speak life over myself. I learned to be mindful of the way I would walk and sit. I believe that it all starts within our mind and how we view ourselves. I once listened to Dr. Monroe saying that a loin is not the biggest or smartest animal in the jungle. The lion, however, has confidence in himself. A loin walks with grace and his head is up when he enters the area of his territory. Over the years, I have listened to a lot of motivational speakers. This act of consistency as well as reading the word of God has helped me in my self-confidence. Praying and mediating on the word of God has helped me find my self-worth. I am grateful for the man of God that spoke over my life for many years and the years of teaching I have received from attending church. I have learned to not only be a hearer of the word of God but a doer of the word of God.

STAGE TWO (LEVEL UP) HAVING SELF-CONFIDENCE

The definition of self-confidence is to believe in oneself and be assured that what you do, whether you fail or winning or losing you are confident that you can continue through as success is an ongoing process.

Do you struggle with self-confidence? If so, today is your day to address this issue in your life.

1. What happens to you emotionally when you feel yourself experiencing lack of confidence?

   a.________________________________

   b.________________________________

   c.________________________________

   d.________________________________

e.______________________________________

2. What are the areas in your life that you feel you are confident in?

   a.______________________________________

   b.______________________________________

   c.______________________________________

   d.______________________________________

   e.______________________________________

3. Who are the confident people you admire?

   a.______________________________________

   b.______________________________________

   c.______________________________________

   d.______________________________________

   e.______________________________________

4. What sometimes happens in your life that causes you to question your confidence?
   a.____

   b.____

   c.____

   d.____

   e.____

5. Are you confident in public speaking, addressing a crowd or a group? If so list the times you had to publicly speak. If you was not confident, list the times when you did not feel confident but had to speak anyway?
   a.____

   b.____

   c.____

   d.____

   e.____

6. Do you see yourself walking into a room with confidence but not arrogance? Where do you plan to go walking in confidence? List the places you desire to walk in confidence in.
   a.______________________________________

   b.______________________________________

   c.______________________________________

   d.______________________________________

   e.______________________________________

7. Name the events. people or places that have once made you feel that you don't have confidence. Once you list them, forgive the situation, the person or yourself and move forward after today.
   a.______________________________________

   b.______________________________________

   c.______________________________________

   d.______________________________________

   e.______________________________________

STAGE THREE

FACING YOUR FEARS

Rock Bottom will teach you lessons that Mountain Tops never could.

-Weslyn Bowers

Facing fear is a challenge that we all will come face to face with. Many things can make us fearful. Fear causes your heart to race, and brings on emotions that can lead to doubt, and not believing in yourself. I experienced a type of fear that we all may have faced before. I was driving home from South Carolina to Savannah leaving one client to go to the next. As a business owner, sometimes you will work sun up to sun down. During the drive I had a flat tire and didn't realize it until there was loud sounds on the road. The tire thumped along and got louder and louder. I pulled over to get myself to safety and assess the damage of the tire. My first reaction was to panic. Instead of panicking, however, I paused in the midst of my fear of being alone on a highway and in need of help and said Jesus help me. I called my husband to come and help me but he didn't answer because he was asleep. The next thing I did was called my caregiver to come down the road and to get me so that I could get some assistance with the tire. It was so dark , and even through the fear of just being on the side of the road I said ,"Lord I know you got this. All things work together for the good of them who love the Lord who are called according to your purpose".

This is the same way we have to face the fear in our lives that would hold us back from accomplishing our goals. You could be all alone, and in a dark place in life struggling to make it from day to day. You could be without the necessary needs and trying to provide for a family. These situations are a dark place that brings on fear. Just as I was stuck on the dark road by myself and called on Jesus to help me, you can do the same in your most desperate times of need.

Sometimes in life we have to take some chances. We must kick fear in the face and do what the Lord has called you to do. He will be with you all the way through whatever you are experiencing. Even in your times where it seems you are trembling with fear because you don't know what the next day will bring in your life.

I received the help I needed that night while I was in the dark with a flat tire. God sent all the necessary help and the vehicle was repaired that night. While I was waiting to get the repairs completed, I heard a well-known song that played and the words said that God was working all things out for my good. The song went on to say that God was intentionally working things out for me. This song ministered to me and I knew it was the Lord speaking to me through the song that he had my back in all things. God is there for us through the simplest and the hardest things.

The Lord will minister words of comfort to us in the most unique ways. The Lord reminds me daily that I am his daughter and that there are a crowd of angels that surround my life. I believe that the angels are surrounding all of us as his children. We have no need to receive the spirit of fear, because this is a spirit that God has not given us according to 2Timothy 1:7. What God has given to us is the precious blood of Jesus to be our protection. God said to me, as the years have passed on, that my business and my life is covered with the blood of Jesus. I believe this and this is my truth.

We should face fear and stay focused. In life we will have mentors, coaches, and family members that will encourage us and give us guidance. This is a good thing. The best thing, however, is to have and to know the voice of God that will lead us to all truth and take away all fear. God will always have our backs when it seems as if our backs are against the wall, We have to trust God and denounce fear so that we can walk into our true calling. Many have wondered and asked the question concerning my life, how did she start her business? How did she make six-figures? How did she do all of these things with no college education? My answer is the same yesterday as it is today. It was only through the grace and mercy of God.

To be a business owner of a company you have to make sacrifices through friends, family and finances. You have to surround yourself with like-minded people. You have to celebrate yourself and give yourself permission to be successful. I learned to call those things that be not as though they were so they could manifest in my life. Face your fears, believe in yourself and speak what you want to see happen.

STAGE THREE (LEVEL UP) FACING YOUR FEARS

We have to face our fears. As human-beings, it is a normal emotion to be afraid. Fear of success, however, can keep you stuck doing the same thing year after year and never advancing to the next level of what you can do to achieve your goals. Naturally , we may have a fear of snakes, spiders or just simply a dark room, but fear of becoming who you were born to be is an emotional hindrance.

1. What are the things that you are naturally afraid of? These can be anything you think of first. Name them below.

   a.________________________________

   b.________________________________

   c.________________________________

   d.________________________________

e.____________________________________

2. Are the fears you listed in question #1 hindering you from achieving success? If there are any write what about these fears and what makes you fear them. Ex:snake (poison, they bite etc.)

   a.____________________________________

   b.____________________________________

   c.____________________________________

   d.____________________________________

   e.____________________________________

Are there fears that you have about going to certain places? Name those places.

a.____________________________________

b.____________________________________

c.____________________________________

d.____________________________________

e.____________________________________

3. How do you plan to address the fear that is hindering you from achieving success?
   a.____
   b.____
   c.____
   d.____
   e.____

4. How long have you been afraid of these fears that have hindered you from achieving success?

   ____

   ____

   ____

   ____

   ____

5. Do you see yourself living without fear that would prevent you from achieving success that is on-going? Name the emotions you would feel

when you experience less of being fearful.

.a.______________________________________

b.______________________________________

c.______________________________________

d.______________________________________

e.______________________________________

6. Name and write five scriptures that would help you to be less fearful and more fearless.

a.______________________________________

b.______________________________________

c.______________________________________

d.______________________________________

e.______________________________________

STAGE FOUR

PURPOSE DRIVEN

To understand purpose and stay aware of your purpose is to know that you must keep going. Never give up while pursuing purpose. Always stay true to yourself until the dream you are hoping and believing God for comes true. No matter how things in your life may look like in the moment, we have to speak it, think it and it will manifest someday. Keep the path that you walk in life clear of confusion and do not allow frustrations to bring you down. Things will eventually will make sense after a while.

I have learned to tell myself that I was born a

leader. You were born to lead and stand out. Always be hungry to feed your mind. Be the lion that is climbing the mountain. It can lead you to a job that supercedes a lot of people that went to college for years. I believe in education, and that we should continue to learn as we develop in our minds and are introduced to new endeavors in our lives. I also believe that those who have not went to college can still be successful in a fulfilling and rewarding career.

I am grateful to God that he has chosen me to be a servant for him. I believe for a time such as this he has chosen me to encourage and to be blessing to His people. I know that this is the driving force behind my purpose and this same force I encourage you to have also.

I love giving people jobs who fit the qualification as a PCA (Patient Care Assistant) or a CNA (Certified

Nursing Assistant). I enjoy and find pleasure in being a blessing to my clients.

Walking in your purpose and being determined can bring challenges. I faced many challenges while being purpose driven going from one process to the next. You will find that people who started with you may not end with you as destiny unfolds. Children of God are called into greatness. It is His purpose that we operate in being intentionally motivated with purpose.

There were times that I worked at a fast food restaurant and I was qualified to do so because I had obtained my G.E.D. My boys were young. As a single mother, I was always made sure I provided for their needs. I not only bought them the things they needed but I bought them the things they wanted. I never complained, and I gave my best work no matter where I was employed.

One key principle that I have learned in life is to never complain about the present moment you are in. There is nothing on this earth that lasts forever. The life we now live will once be memories and our spirit goes on to our father in heaven. Just as life comes and goes so will a season of depression, lack of hope, lack of confidence and lack of zeal to pursue purpose. These things will past away once we set our mind on achieving and not complaining.

God will bring us into our set season of His favor. Our position is to speak and believe that there is a set season that God has for us that will come and we will see the flow of favor operate in our lives. Through our times of processing from one stage to the next we do not have to discuss our tests or trials with others. People may be in disagreement with your purpose and the flow of favor on your life. Your ability to sit back and watch our father's will take place in your life should bring the best praise from your heart. God has a way of blessing us in the presence of our enemies and give them access to see His glory on our lives. This is the stage of being purpose driven. To know, to sense, and to understand that your drive does not come from the applause of people but from the approval of God.

STAGE FOUR (LEVEL UP) PURPOSE DRIVEN

Purpose is the reason for which something is done or created. Let's focus on the part that says the reason for which something is created. You were created for a reason. The beauty of being created is that sometimes we know our purpose from the day. We develop into speaking or walking and then there are times where we are revealed our purpose over the course of a life-time.

Have you ever seen a toddler that loved music, drums or keyboards? The toddler didn't become bored with the instruments but continued on year after year asking for the same toy, but maybe more advanced?

This toddler knew his/her purpose very earlier on and continued in that lane of development. This is what we all must do at some point within our lives,. We must continue in the lane given to us.

1. What are some of your favorite things to do?

a.____________________________________

b.____________________________________

c.____________________________________

d.____________________________________

e.____________________________________

2. Do you remember the things you were most interested in at a very earlier age? Name those below.

a.____________________________________

b.____________________________________

c.____________________________________

d.____________________________________

e.______________________________________

3. What have you pursued or is currently pursuing in life to" Master" your gifts, talents and abilities?
   a.______________________________________

   b.______________________________________

   c.______________________________________

   d.______________________________________

   e.______________________________________

4. Have you set goals to become better at achieving the purpose given to you? Name those goals below.
   a.______________________________________

   b.______________________________________

   c.______________________________________

   d.______________________________________

   e.______________________________________

5. What continues to drive you to pursue your purpose in life? Name them below.
   a.______________________________________

b.____

c.____

d.____

e.____

6. Who are the people that pushes you to pursue your purpose?

a.____

b.____

c.____

d.____

e.____

STAGE FIVE

BELIEVE IN YOURSELF

You must believe in yourself. I had to learn to take the limitations off the way I was thinking. I began to desire wanting a better environment and atmosphere to live in. I soon realized over time that the only person who can hold me back was myself. I started asking myself questions such as," Do you have what it takes, Carolyn to be a CEO of a homecare business?" I revisited my entire life through thoughts. I envisioned how I cared about businesses where I worked when I was employed, as if it were my own, It should never be about you when doing a job. You should always want to be a team player. You should always desire to see the team do great and not just yourself. I have always wanted more out of life. I call this way of believing as leveling up your thinking. We all think and have faith on different levels. Each person level of thinking can change but never get stuck in one way without advancing into the new things you can achieve and do. In order for me to believe in myself I had to connect myself to positive and influential people.

The most positive person is my life was my mother. I have learned that having a good mother is the best positivity you can have in your life. My mother taught me that I should not be in other people's business. For this reason she taught me to learn to stay in my own lane and purpose as it relates to living a peaceful and productive life. I had to learn to not compare myself with others and say to myself that I was good enough even with a GED. I no longer accepted being Mediocre as a comfortable way of life anymore. I had to make up in my mind I was going to be unstoppable in every area of my life. I prayed to God for more wisdom everyday to help me accomplish my goals. I knew there would be times that it would not be easy so I prayed that the Lord would help me in every area of my life as a business person. I stop thinking I was less than enough and began thinking that I was more than enough.

I have been created and called. My Lord and Savior Jesus handpicked me for such a time as this to be a encourager and mentor to those who would receive what he has placed within me. This is the same mindset you must take on to believe in yourself. Each morning say to yourself that you are chosen and not forsaken. You are who God says you are.

I also learned discipline. I knew that arising early in

the morning and staying up late at night would eventually pay off when others were asleep. I get up early to think of a master plan. I prayed that God would granted me the wisdom on how to help others and become better in everything that I would put my hands to do. Skills of being successful are built this way. I learned by educating myself and listening to great motivational speakers 30 minutes a day.

You have to believe in yourself because no one going to want your dream as hard as you want your dreams. You must stay focused. Never become distracted or hindered by what others think or say about you. You have to give your all, or give nothing, in order to accomplish great achievements. I can recall many times I wanted to give up because I failed at different things. I didn't realize it then but my failures were pushing me to greatness. You have to know that at times you will fall but you can't stay down. You have to get up. Always be determined to get back in the race. The word of God according to the book of Ecclesiastes 9:11 declares, the race isn't given to the swift, neither is it given to the strong. So hold your head up and get back in the race called life. Tell yourself, "Yes I can". Speak words that give life to you like CPR. Every day you will began to see and know you have victory in your life and you will fill so great on the inside. No one can take this away form you unless you give them permission to. I challenge you to find out what you're good at doing and start doing (CPR), to your hopes and dreams. Faith is the key that will open every door. I believe in you so it is time that you start believing in you!

STAGE FIVE (LEVEL UP) BELIEVE IN YOURSELF

Some people say believing is seeing. But when you are purpose driven you believe even when you don't see. The best "ah ha" moment you can have is the moment you achieve something that you thought you could not do.

1. What are five achievements in your life that you thought you could not do but was able to do after you believed in yourself?

a.______________________________________

b.______________________________________

c.______________________________________

d.______________________________________

e.______________________________________

What are some of the steps you took achieving the goals in your life that you didn't' see yourself doing?

a.____

b.____

c.____

d.____

e.____

2. Do you believe there are other things you can achieve in your life that you have not yet tried to pursue? Name them below.

a.____

b.____

c.____

d.____

e.____

3. Who are the people you have watched believe in themselves? Name them below.

   a.____

   b.____

   c.____

   d.____

   e.____

4. What steps did you see these people take that you were aware of to achieve their goals?

   a.____

   b.____

   c.____

   d.____

   e.____

5. What are the areas or situations that have occurred in your life that have hindered you from believing in yourself?

a.____

b.____

c.____

d.____

e.____

6. Write five inspirational quotes from people you know, people you don't, or famous people that have inspired you.

a.____

b.____

c.____

d.____

e.____

STAGE SIX

LIGHT WEIGHT VS HEAVY WEIGHT

It's time to let the light weight of small minded matters go. The small and irrelevant things like gossiping, envy, jealousy, razor-sharp tongue, unpleasant speaking, cutting a bitter tongue and a fearful spirit are many things that have to be removed from our lives. You must keep in mind that these light-weight spirits can keep you from walking in your heavy-weight calling. God has called you for greatness and you cannot allow light-weight matters to stop you anymore.

I remember years ago sitting on the telephone for hours gossiping about what others may have been wearing and doing. I discussed things that had no value to my life or the person who listened to this conversation and also communicated with me on those matters. I'm so grateful for my husband today. He always would tell me, "Mind your own business Carolyn Milton, and stay in your own lane", he would say in a high pitched voice.

Sometimes we need people to help us with ridding ourselves of the light-weight matters in our life. We may not realize how light weight issues are negative spirits that can hinder our destiny.

The times that I would sit on the telephone communicating about unnecessary matters was unproductive to my life. I could have utilized that time to search for resources to help my business, obtain new business ideas or helping someone in need. This type of dead weight in your life can keep you from your accomplishments. Sometimes, we are also dealing with emotional hindrances such as resentments bitterness, disappointments, anger, and pain. These light weight situations can have you walking around with a bad "flavor" about yourself. Having this type of weight causes others to reject you. People who could be a help to you and in your life will turn from you because of an negative attitude.

This past year, I began to place myself into an arena with heavy weight champions. I decided to invest in the different seminars and workshops within my city and surrounding areas. I knew it was time for me to take my mindset and the way I think about success to another level. This adjustment is needed in the life of anyone who is striving for success. I keep a wonderful group of successful people in my corner, because I knew that God had also called me to be a "heavy weight champion" in this earth for success.

In order to become who God has called you to be in this earth, the old mindset of limitations must be released from your life.

I've learned over the years, whatever it is that you desire to achieve and become in life takes time and change. You have to change and surround yourself with people of the same status. Change your circle of influence and open your mind to heavy weight goals. I have learned that successful people are not gifted. They just work hard and strive to succeed on purpose.

When you let go of light weights, you learn to celebrate others success or accomplishments. Focus on being a heavy weight champion that can also influence others to be successful. Embrace and celebrate change. Life will always bring about new changes.

Having light weights in your life can have you feeling lonely as if you have to be around others all the time or in need of someone always being in your corner. You can learn to enjoy yourself being alone in a positive way. I call this "Carolyn's time", to help me evaluate my life. This is the time I can remove all toxins from my life through prayer, study and meditation. Remove the light weights from your life, so you can discover the God gifted purpose in your life.

STAGE SIX (LEVEL UP) LIGHT WEIGHT VS HEAVY WEIGHT

Everyone can't go where you are going. This is your time to reflect on where you see yourself going as it relates to your vision. Now that you have been informed on this matter, let's level up with vision to accomplish heavy weight goals.

1. What are the visions you have for your life, career, or family ? You may have more than one. Write them below.

    a.________________________________

    b.________________________________

    c.________________________________

    d.________________________________

    e.________________________________

2. What are the many reasons you live for? Write them below.
   a.______________________________________
   b.______________________________________
   c.______________________________________
   d.______________________________________
   e.______________________________________

3. Where do you see yourself going in life.
   a.______________________________________
   b.______________________________________
   c.______________________________________
   d.______________________________________
   e.______________________________________

4. How do you want to be known?
   a.______________________________________

b.____

c.____

d.____

e.____

5. What are the light- weights that would hinder your vision. Write them below.
   a.____

b.____

c.____

d.____

e.____

6. What are the heavy-weight goals you would like to achieve? How long would it take you to achieve these goals?

a.____

b.____

c.____

d.____

e.____

STAGE SEVEN

BE VALUABLE

See yourself as a wonderful and amazing person. I began to see myself in this way and it gave me strength. Having this strength gave me the ability to succeed in accomplishments that seemed too much for me to achieve. I had a GED for many years and I allowed what I thought about a GED meant to cripple me. I learned to know that God handpicked me from birth out of my mother's womb. We have to remember God created greatness in you from birth. He has spoken to me through his word that not only am I fearfully and wonderfully made but so are you. I have his fingerprint and his DNA, inside of my spiritual make-up.

I remember the year when I was a student at Alfred E. Beach High School. I was in what is called the OPT program. This program helped me to prepare for my GED. I felt like I was nothing because I wasn't in the regular classes. This was the mindset that I carried because I didn't see my success in the stage I was in. Sometimes in life, your thoughts can process things as if you are a failure. These thoughts will try to make you feel less than others. It is very important that these thoughts be released from your mind so that you can further succeed. You have to know deep within yourself that you are qualified and approved by God. No one can discredit what God has created on the inside of you. I started thinking and speaking that I am valuable because God created me .

There is greatness on the inside of each of us that makes us feel extremely valuable. This greatness is the connection to our success and purpose in life. I feel so wealthy because I have discovered my worth. I know who I am, and why I'm here. I am walking in my purpose. I am The apple of my father's eye in heaven. It does not matter what others think of you or me, as long as you are living according to the will of God. Their opinion of us shouldn't matter to us. Just keep your head up and keep growing and glowing in God. Watch him let us shine like a diamond through your life.

God created you. No one can stop you from becoming who he has called you to be unless you allow them to stop you. Sometimes thinking about the emotional hurts of the past can bring back unwanted memories. People who are vindictive and have malicious motives can also bring up the past with the purpose to cause harm. Do not allow the past to hinder you or keep you from experiencing your winning season that God has assigned just for you. My assignment with this book is to give you words of life and encouragement. You are valuable.

You and I are free from living in the past memories of failures. I once heard a great leader and motivational speaker say that the mind is the battle ground of Satan. With this knowledge, I have learned to speak positive affirmations over my sons and I.

We are overcomers by the word of our testimonies. We are victors, and more than conquerors! I am more spiritually stronger today than I have ever been. If you can remember that you are valuable and full of wealth, you can continue to experience the wisdom, and joy of the Lord every day.

STAGE SEVEN (LEVEL UP) BE VALUABLE

You are valuable to those who love you and even to the people who have not met you. Once you have been introduced to anyone, you have the opportunity to reveal your worth and value in their life. What a blessing it is to know that your value is worth meeting.

1. Do you believe that you have a positive influence on those in your inner circle or immediate family? Write how you share your positive influences below.

    a.________________________________

    b.________________________________

    c.________________________________

    d.________________________________

    e.________________________________

2. What are some of the valuable gifts you have within you that you can share with the world?

   a.____________________________________

   b.____________________________________

   c.____________________________________

   d.____________________________________

   e.____________________________________

3. Who are the people in your life that you value?

   a.____________________________________

   b.____________________________________

   c.____________________________________

   d.____________________________________

   e.____________________________________

4. What is it about their lives that brings value to your life?

   a.____________________________________

b.____

c.____

d.____

e.____

5. How can you allow your gifts to bring value into the lives of others?

   a.____

   b.____

   c.____

   d.____

   e.____

6. If you can place value on your life what would you compare it to? Ex: diamonds, pearls, dollar amounts...List them below

   a.____

   b.____

   c.____

d.____

e.____

STAGE EIGHT

GIFTS WILL OPEN DOORS

Life can be taken for granted when the appreciation for life is dishonored. At times, the gifts we possess can be taken for granted and we miss the opportunity to be a blessing or to be blessed by someone else. It's very important that we take the time to learn ourselves and our God-given gifts.

We have gifts that are within us that needs to be discovered. These gifts and abilities can open doors of opportunities for us, and expose us to accomplish even greater achievements in our lives. Many times, we are pursuing our passion for things we desire to do, instead of cultivating our gifts. At times, pursuing passion can become exhausting. Exhaustion comes when you are not using your gifts that come naturally. Forcing yourself to do something that you may enjoy doing, but not gifted to do, can become tiresome. Cultivating your gifts and pursuing it with purpose can produce success in the end.

You must make sure that the gift that you have been graced to receive is used. It does not matter if it is one gift that you are good at doing. Take the gift that you have and use it to bring glory to God. There are endless possibilities that your gift can take you to. For example, if you are gifted to frying chicken then you fry the heck out of that chicken! Use your gift of cooking to bring glory to God, by giving back to those in need and watch that gift prosper. Your ability to fry chicken can produce millions of dollars. If you don't believe me, google Kentucky Fried Chicken owner (Colonel Sanders). He started a restaurant on the side of the road in North Corbin, Kentucky, during the great depression. Mr. Colonel Sanders was at the age of 40 when he became famous around the world for his chicken. Colonel Sanders, believed in himself, and the gift he had been given.

Stop doubting yourself. The gift you have been given is never to be compared to anyone else's gift. Your gift is awaiting for you to fulfill its greatest potential. It is inside of you, pursuing the opportunity to be revealed. Your God given gift is given for you to pursue your purpose in life. It can make room for you to be a blessing to others, and open doors no man can shut.

Testimony:

I remember receiving a message at the very start of my business. There was a man of God that spoke a message to me saying, " Use what you got in your hand". From that day forward, I would pray and ask God to help me find myself, and to know the call that was placed upon my life. The thought of my purpose came to my remembrance when I was working for a company called Grisworld. There was a lady that needed her back massaged. She had been in so much pain. I took the time to rub her back, because I wanted to help her through the pain she was experiencing. After I massaged her back she informed me that her pain had actually went away. The lady said to me that I had in my possession healing hands. There are times when I think about what she said to me. This encourages me to continue to care and show compassion to others.

There was also another time that one of my clients passed out and I called 911. I remember staying calm and knew that I could not panic in this situation that I was placed in. I talked stayed on the phone with the operator until the EMS arrived. While waiting for the emergency team, I continued to rub her hands and prayed, calling on the name of Jesus the entire time. I watched as I continued to pray the lady eyes began to open. The EMS quickly came. Once they were on the scene they informed me that I did great by staying calm and not leaving the patient. The emergency team checked her vital, which were normal. They informed me that she must have just blacked out. She refused to go to the hospital, I did not try to force her because it was her right. When the EMS team left, I suddenly just knew that God had called me to care for the seniors. From that day forward, I cared for this client. She appreciated my love and compassion of the services I rendered to her.

Eventually the company I worked for at the time went out of business. I knew I was going to become a business owner in the field of homecare, because I had the gift of caring. I loved my job and I did it to the glory of God. I started out as a CNA and now I have employees that share the same compassion and care towards those who need the services that we provide. Using what I have in my hands through the gift of caring, has been a blessing. I do not like to brag about helping others, but I feel there is a time to share what you are able to do to provide service to others. I do know that the things we do in secret or privately, God will allow the greater rewards to manifest for us before others. This happens only so his glory is revealed through our lives. I know this to be true that blessing others will opening doors of blessing to come your way.

I've noticed over the years that many times people say they are a BOSS. A famous rapper by the name of Rick Ross said in one of his songs. *"A boss is someone who guarantee the staff going to eat not someone standing on their own feet".* I had learn in order to be a Boss you have to be a blessing and always be selfless . You have to always make sure payroll is in the bank. I learned being a CEO requires me to be disciplined in many areas of my life. A BOSS is also a giver and this ability of being a CEO has opened many avenues of God allowing my gift to cultivate and blossom. I say to you, find your gifts and let God do the re

STAGE EIGHT (LEVEL UP) GIFTS WILL OPEN DOORS

Do you know that you were born with a gift? Have you thought or considered what is your true gift from God?. This is the time in your life to release your gift. Allow the gift(s) to be revealed as you follow through the questions below. Your time of manifestation can be right now and the next door is right down the hallway.

1. Name several of the gifts that you know you have been born to do.

   a.________________________________

   b.________________________________

   c.________________________________

   d.________________________________

   e.________________________________

2. Have you considered the doors that you would like to see opened for you because of gifts that you possess.
   a.____________________________________
   b.____________________________________
   c.____________________________________
   d.____________________________________
   e.____________________________________

3. If you are not operating in your gifts, are there doors of opportunities that have been closed? Name those doors below.
   a.____________________________________
   b.____________________________________
   c.____________________________________
   d.____________________________________
   e.____________________________________

4. Have you created a goal for your gift to be cultivated and to be released? If not name the long and short term goals for you to allow your gift to be used to bring God glory.
   a.____
   b.____
   c.____
   d.____
   e.____

5. Who are the people that have always seen that you have a gift, and what doors did God use them to open for you because of your gift?
   a.____
   b.____
   c.____
   d.____
   e.____

6. Who would you like to encourage that you noticed has a similar gift that you have? How can you help to mentor/train them in the way of being a blessing to others, through the gifts given to them.
   a.______________________________________
   b.______________________________________
   c.______________________________________
   d.______________________________________
   e.______________________________________

STAGE NINE BECOMING A CEO

I've learned over the years and even until this day that you have to set healthy boundaries with clients and employees. This is very critical for your business. Setting a standards from the start and continuing with the standards of excellence from across the board makes a successful and professional company. As a business person it is important that you have contracts that are up-to-date and in order as it relates to your business. Build a team of excellent team workers and remember to always be respectful to everyone that is connected to the business. Giving respecting is one of my key points while serving as a CEO. Sometimes others will not understand some of the decisions that you will have to make as a CEO. This is to be expected, however, you must always be wise and having knowledge of where your business is headed. You have to remember it's your vision and the decisions that you are making is the best for everyone within the business. If you always keep this in mind you will be okay. The best advice that I can give, that is the most important key in my business is always do what you do to give glory to God. This type of mindset keeps me humble and full of humility toward the people.

I have been graced to be a CEO of two companies. The name of my cleaning company is Handle with Loving Care Cleaning Services LLC . I have owned this company since 2018, but was afraid to launch the beginning start dates until this year of 2019. My son Marquis J. Williams manages this company with excellence and class.

There comes a destined time in our lives where we have to tell fear you no longer live here. I made the decision to kick fear out of my decisions and since then the company has been doing great. It has been a blessing to have my son managing this business. Marquis was applying for jobs and he seem to never get an opened door of opportunity. The doors where closing for my son obtaining a good job. I had a sit down talk with him and said, " Hey son, if these doors keep closing you got to build your own door now". This meant it was time for me to invest in business with my son, and teach him the skills of success that I have learned. It was also my time to teach him that he too could learn the power of entrepreneurship, and obtain his own company. He was determine not to allow his past mistakes to hunt him down and reverse his future. I taught him that people may never forgive us for our mistakes, but God does. We must take each day, step by step and trust God as we trust the process.

My second business is Handle With Loving Care Homecare LLC. This company is my first baby in business. You can't tell me God isn't good. From a GED to CEO is who I am. We have to realize it is the great master who we should put our in trust in as he gives us the gifts to function on this earth. We can only strive daily to do his will, but there are times you and I will fall short of following his instructions. We all have flaws, and you will make mistakes. I am not painting a picture of a perfect life. I do what I can to build my relationship with God daily. I often ask God to help me stay the course of doing good and serving others. There are times where you will experience times getting hard and it's not always going to be easy. It can seem even harder when there are many people watching your every move and looking to you for answers. If you always remain humble you will be able to exceed and experience more times of celebration in your business than disappointments. My view point of a CEO is always let Jesus be your CEO. You will always be a great CEO in the eyesight of God, no matter what others may think of you.

Being a CEO is not an easy profession. A ballerina dances with grace and elegance, but behind this beauty there has been much work, skill and practice that has been placed upon the dancer. In their time of practice no one knew the pain, days of tiredness, the soreness in their feet that the dancer had to endure. The audience only see the dance. This is the same with successful people. Many will not see your struggle but they will see your success. So many times I wanted to throw in the towel. I could not give up so easily. I had to press and push until the chains broke. I had to accept the chains of hindrances to fall off of me, so that I could be free. It was a must that I be who God has created me to be. The Lord knows my heart. I am happy for others with titles, but I'm not big on titles for myself. I have learned that titles can make people think more highly of themselves than they should.

High-minded people can seem to forget that love should always be given and begin to mistreat others. I have seen this happen and it breaks my heart when these actions are displayed in the lives of people who I may have once looked up to. Titles can bring on the wrong spirit, and that spirit is called pride. I love to be a servant. I strive daily to be humble. I never like being called Boss, CEO or even Mrs. Milton. I have learned that these titles given to me is the respect that is being shown for who I am and what I have accomplished.

It suddenly dawned on me one day after speaking with a lady from the IRS that I had to address myself with a title. The lady from the IRS asked me what was my title in the organization, while speaking business with her over the line concerning my account. My response was I am the CEO. After I hung up the phone tears began to flow down my cheeks from my eyes. I heard a clear voice from GOD speak to me and he said. *"You earned this title and you didn't go to college for this one baby. You went through so many years of trials and tribulations behind closed doors"*.

Others may never understand the struggles you have endured in life. They may never know your hurt, pain, and disappointments. Your focus is to be sure that you have an understanding of who you are, and things will work out for you every time.

I can remember the times that I would quickly leave church while in service and other different events, because no one showed up to the jobs. I would have to immediately leave from where I was, or what I was doing to work the cases for my clients. That's when I realized God had called me for something bigger than myself. I knew that serving senior citizens was a gift and a servanthood God had given to me. A still voice would always speak to me and say, "*well-done daughter, you went to the school of theology to be excellent in serving*". I learn from Bishop Odum and my dad that serving people is serving God. I know that I have earned the title of CEO with blood, sweat, and tears. Many days I was the topic of discussion for the very people I was helping, but I also learned Jesus was talked about while he was doing the Father's will. He never allowed anyone to stop him from pursuing and accomplishing his purpose here on earth. People may never understand why you do what you do, They may never understand your vision. I encourage you to never give up. I never gave up my vision, no matter what I experienced and what situation may have occurred. I have enjoyed being a blessing to others by offering them an opportunity by obtaining a job. When I do what God has purposed me to do then I know that God has used me as his servant. God can do anything he desires and if I don't do as he has commanded, he can use the next person to fulfill his purpose here on earth through their life. I just love giving God glory in the midst of it all. I can hear my Father in Heaven saying to me. *"keep up the good work CEO Carolyn Milton".*

STAGE NINE BECOMING A CEO

(LEVEL UP!)

YOUR BUSINESS

Doing Business you need to know about your industry or Company:

1. Requirements and what will it take for your business to start.
2. The products needed for your business
3. The needs you can provide
4. Who will you serve?

The purpose of business not about the number of dollars made, but it is about the number of lives changed!

KNOW IT WELL, DEEPLY AND INTIMATELY!

Business Tip

- God First (Jesus is my CEO)
- Be clear in your vision
- I want you to be skillful, clear and dedicated to your business
- Stay focused to always win
- While you pursue further education always score high on test scores. This allows you to gets the best careers and get the best scholarships.
- Balance in your life

THE LAWS OF VISIONS

The Law:

And the LORD answered me, and said, Write the vision, and make it plain upon tables, that he may run that read it.

-Habakkuk 2:2

Vision:

This is where the company CEO would like to see the future of the business. The mission to see the company succeed and how the business will grow and be known.

Ask yourself

What is your vision?

What do you live for?

Where do you want to go ?

How do you want to be known?

IT'S YOUR CHOICE!

COACH CAROLYN MILTON

Carolyn E. Milton is Married to Allen W. Milton, the proud mother of two sons Daniel and Marquis, she is a servant of the Lord in his kingdom. She is the CEO of Handle with Loving Care LLC of Georgia and South Carolina, with over 35 employees that she respects so much. She is the founder of "Save A Life from Ebola" where she raised funds to help a family back in Nigeria in 2015. She is the Founder of "Teens Will Conquer Success" and she is a Homecare Coach. She inspires others to become great leaders in their own personal lives as well as the business world of entrepreneurs. In Carolyn's spare time she loves to motivate individuals from day to day on social media.

Notes

Made in the
USA
Columbia, SC

82224247R00055